TRAINING CONTRACT/ SOLICITOR

*GET ONE/
BECOME ONE*

Nicola Mead-Batten

For Teifi
Who believed in me

Contents

Chapter 1 Starting Your (And This) Story 1

Chapter 2 Is The Law Right For You? 7

Chapter 3 The Right Law Firm? 29

Chapter 4 The Application 46

Chapter 5 The Interview 70

Preparation, Preparation, Preparation… 86

And Finally, Here's To Your Future! 101

CHAPTER 1
STARTING YOUR (AND THIS) STORY

In my experience, life is a series of "light bulb" moments or "spots of time" (according to William Wordsworth). The moment when that complicated algebra formula makes sense; when you meet that special someone. The light bulb moment when you work out what you want to do with your life. They come in all shapes and sizes, strike you when you least expect it and aren't generally 'one offs' - you may meet more than one special someone or figure out what you want to do with your life several times over!

Every so often in my working life (maybe every few weeks or months) I still get "spots of time" (some big and some little ones) when I get a new business idea, or I get beneath the skin of a client's business and start to understand the way they work, or I find a common interest with an individual which really gives you something to talk about in an otherwise seemingly artificial (and occasionally quite awkward) networking situation.

The decision to write this book was one such moment. I've been practising law for eleven years. Before that I studied it for about five. That's sixteen years playing this field. My work gives me the opportunity for some creative output, of sorts. As a litigator, I (personally) see some creativity in developing a compelling case theory to win your case (sad, I know). But there has always been some part of me which wanted to create something of my own. I enjoy writing and, cheesy as it may sound, I get a kick out of sharing the benefit of my experiences – good and bad – with others, particularly more junior lawyers, and they seem (on the surface at least!) to respond positively to my advice.

I was having a conversation with my husband about one encounter with a more junior lawyer who I had worked with since she was a trainee and had just risen to Senior Associate in my firm. It was my last day at the firm after nine years. It was very emotional and I was going into all my wonderful ex-colleagues' offices to say "goodbye". She came to my office in tears and said a huge "thank you" for what I had done for her personally and professionally over a number of years. She said that she 'owed' me so much and would not forget me in a hurry. I was pretty overwhelmed by such high praise, especially from someone like her. I said to my husband that I felt inspired and really wanted to condense what I'd learned in my career so far into a series of short books – starting with "how to get the training contract you want" (or something with the same content but a snazzier title!). He said "why not?" and that was that. Eureka!

Why not indeed?! What a question! What I haven't mentioned is that, as well as working full time in a challenging and occasionally pretty stressful job (in fact, a new job which I started two years ago, in a new country – well, sort of – read on...) I'm also a mum to three year old twins. Not much time for writing books really. But I'm a complete pain when I get an idea in my head and so here it is.

Another big light bulb moment in my life was my decision to become a lawyer in the first place. If I'm honest, it was more of a series of moments (if that's not a total contradiction in terms?) which, twenty years on, sort of morph in to one. I was (and in fairness, still am) obsessed with legal dramas – usually American movies: *Philadelphia*; *A Few Good Men; The Firm; The Pelican Brief; Kramer v Kramer* (now S*uits*, *The Good Wife* etc etc). I genuinely believed that this was what lawyers did on a day to day basis: sought the truth (*"you can't handle the truth!"*), believed in justice (*"what I love the most about the law? ...It's that, every now and* *again...not often but occasionally...you get to be a part of justice being done. It really is quite a thrill when that happens..."*), and fought court room battle after court room battle. It's slightly more complicated than that and involves a lot more pen-pushing than I expected but I do enjoy going to court, especially when I believe my client is going to win (which, strangely enough, is pretty much all of the time!)!

I also had an inspirational teacher who when I said – initially somewhat flippantly – that I wanted to be a lawyer, took every step in his power to make that happen: from organising for ex-pupils who had become solicitors to come in to speak to me to facilitating work experience at a high street firm – for no reason other than to help me get where I wanted to go.

Once these seemingly small triggers were set in motion there was no going back and I effectively created my own self-fulfilling prophecy.

Fast forward to studying law at the University of Warwick in 2000 and, during a law fair in my second year, I met a trainee solicitor from Baker McKenzie who, despite my rather dishevelled appearance (I was wearing a parka jacket and had purple hair) took the time to tell me how much she loved her job. I can't even remember her name (although I did note it at the time) but she was actually a pretty significant person in my life. I applied to Baker McKenzie for a training contract (amongst others – as explained later in the book) and the rest, as they say, is history. I spent nine years in the London office of Baker McKenzie (and one in Melbourne, Australia), qualifying into the Dispute Resolution team, before moving (after having my children) back "home" to Cardiff, south Wales, and joining (what I believe to be a great young firm) Capital Law in 2015.

There were a few "spots of time" in that paragraph which I've developed throughout the book.

The purpose of this Chapter is to set the scene for the remainder of this book. The book is quite short. That's deliberate. It could have been hundreds of pages long. But that's not what you need. You need a book which gives an honest and useful guide to making an application which might just set you on the road to a great career in the law. The idea that this book could be a small part in helping just one person makes all the effort in writing it seem unquestionably worthwhile. I feel well-placed to provide this advice because I'm sufficiently long in the tooth(!) and have met enough great people along the way to pick up a few 'tricks' by osmosis but am not so far removed from the process of making a training contract application (or, indeed, being a trainee) that I've forgotten what it's like to be in that position. I've also drawn on colleagues and friends' thoughts (lawyers and those in Legal HR) along the way...

Ultimately what I believe is that you need to be conscious of your own light bulb moments. The moment(s) you decided to embark on a career in the law (if, indeed, you've made that decision for certain – you may well still be waiting for it, there's no shame in that), the moment you chose to go to your University or picked your degree subject, or the moment you felt inspired when travelling or listening to music, reading or playing sport. I guess what I'm trying to say is: know who you are and use it as effectively as possible. If you take nothing else away from this book, remember that and you can't go far wrong…

<u>CHAPTER 2</u>
IS THE LAW RIGHT FOR YOU?

This isn't a rhetorical question. Yes, you've picked up this book and so you may be thinking "of course, the law is right for me. I wouldn't have bought this book if it wasn't!" But let's explore that question for just a minute. Do you have doubts? If so, what are they? Are you considering other options? Are you thinking about a career in the law just because you are doing a law degree and so it seems like the natural course? Or are you not doing a law degree and wondering if you want to venture into the unknown? Or have you always known that you wanted a career in the law?

Write the answers to these questions down. It may be the most important thing you do in the course of applying for a Training Contract. The automated nature of internet based applications often means that individual applicants overlook the essential reasons that they're making an application in the first place. I've seen numerous applications – some of which have been successful in winning training contracts at one of the world's biggest law firms - and even many of these are often fundamentally flawed in this respect. The applications lack imagination and they're often dull as hell. I'm not suggesting that you write a ditty or swallow a thesaurus when you get writing - quite the opposite in fact. But one thing you need is to tell a story: why are you applying for a training contract? Why become a lawyer? Why are you right for the law? Why is the law right for you? Grab a pen and paper and write this down in the most illustrative form possible.

I often find this is best done by way of a "mind-map". Ever come across mind-maps before? I hadn't until quite recently but now I'm hooked. They're incredibly simple but very accessible and creative ways of recording your thoughts about a topic. You may even find them useful in your future revision exercises. For a really illustrative example, check out http://thinkbuzan.com/. You can get a free trial at this website of mind-map software but you don't have to get this technical. They're basically creative ways of working out what the big issues or messages you want to get across are in an almost skeleton form and then add the "limbs" or meat to the bones. Let's start a mindmap with how I made the decision to pursue a career in law. All of my mindmaps are contained in the "Appendix" to this book. The first one – why I made the decision to pursue a career in law in **Mindmap #1**

What does yours look like?

I was a determined sort: determined to overcome apparent barriers to my success including a careers adviser at my State School who suggested joining the Police as an alternative to becoming a lawyer and handed me a GNVQ in Health and Social Care recommendation despite predictions of stellar grades in my GCSEs. Working class kids just didn't stand a chance in becoming solicitors, she implied. I was drawn to performance and debate but, equally, I loved science - forensic analysis and exploration. My favourite subject at school was Chemistry. At the time I didn't know how the mix of attributes I was displaying at 15/16 could give me such an interesting and varied story to talk about when trying to get the job of my dreams at 23/24. This exercise helped me to see it.

In my view, it's a crucial first step in preparing to write your application, and we'll keep coming back to it in the rest of the book. So keep it handy.

The pathway to becoming a solicitor

Many students don't know about the essential education you need to be a lawyer/ solicitor. Well, from an England and Wales perspective, and at time of going to press, there are 3 core routes:

ROUTE 1

Undergraduate Law Degree (typically a "LLB" degree although it can be BA/ BSc, particularly when you study joint honours with Law)

- Legal Practice Course ("LPC")

Attending Law School to undertake the shortest route to post-graduate qualification to make you 'Training Contract ready': all you'll need after you've undertaken the LPC is two years (or, in some cases where you've undertaken work as a paralegal, for example – less) of a Training Contract and (subject to regulatory approval) you're good to go.

The LPC is what it says on the tin: it's about practising the law. I remember my first lecture at Law School. The lecturer said "this is not your last year as a student [cue a few cheeky smiles in the room], but your first as a practitioner!" Cheesy as it was, it resonated with me. You pick your electives based around what you're hoping to practise (mine were Corporate ones chosen for me by Baker McKenzie) alongside your "core" subjects of Solicitors Accounts Rules/ Conduct Rules/ Litigation (Criminal/ Civil), Property and Business Law & Practice. A lot of the learning will be done on your own. You're post-grads and grown-ups of course! The remainder of the sessions will be conducted via lectures and seminars – much like your undergraduate studies.

What a fair number of people don't know is that some firms – usually London based and/or the most prestigious or long-standing – offer to pay your fees for undertaking the LPC. Some even pay your fees and give you a living subsidy so that your attendance at Law School is effectively free. That's some incentive when, after some of you will have tens of thousands of pounds worth of student debt, you can add another £10-15k at least to that figure. I was a fortunate enough beneficiary of such a programme. I thought at the time that, if I hadn't been, I probably wouldn't have gone to Law School but I've since met numerous people that weren't so lucky, who pulled their sleeves up, took on further debt but have since paid it back and now have very fulfilling well-paid jobs.

One of the reasons I ask the above question is because it's an expensive process if your heart isn't set on the end product. That said, being a patron of the law is always an impressive thing to have on one's CV even if it isn't where you ultimately end up in five, ten or twenty years down the line.

ROUTE 2

Undergrad degree in *Anything*…

- Conversion Course (CPE/ GDL) AND THEN

The "Common Professional Examination" or "Graduate Diploma in Law" is the connector between a non-law degree and the LPC. Non-lawyers often worry that they'll be at a disadvantage to law students when fighting for training contracts. It's simply not the case. Firms value the diversity non-lawyers offer their firms and there are many areas of the law where having an alternative undergraduate pathway is arguably a better string to one's bow than starting studying law at 18, e.g.:

Science graduates often make excellent intellectual property lawyers – particularly patent attorneys. I know a number that work with University start-ups in helping them to patent their latest innovations

Tax and pensions specialists often have a background in mathematics. They're some of the most revered in the business: areas of law which require fantastic intellect and an analytical brain.

History/ humanities are fairly common backgrounds for litigators, in my experience. Perhaps it's the requirement to have a forensic, analytical brain that's capable of remembering facts, dates, and to tell stories (or case theories) in a compelling way.

The trick when it comes to selling yourself and embarking on a legal career is being able to explain your choice of non-law degree. No one's expecting a bright-eyed 17 year old choosing their degree to have all the answers but you will need to explain why you made the choice you did at this young age and why it stands you in good stead for a legal career now.

You may even be reading this book considering embarking on a second career. Again, there's a lot to sell here. I've come across a number of fantastic lawyers who have had interesting careers earlier in their lives from spies to scientists, accountants to archaeologists and everything in between. I'm always sat in awe listening to what they've done before and why they chose to embark on a legal career later in life. You have an incredible story to tell in the course of your application.

- LPC

See above!

<u>ROUTE 3</u>

The CILEx route: I have to confess, I didn't know much about this option until I met my colleague Lucy Emanuel – who amazes me every day. So I asked her to explain how it works:

> *"First you need to become a qualified legal executive or a fellow of CILEX. To do this you must complete the academic training. This will incorporate completion of 'Level 3'*

training (2 years part time) unless you are exempt. After that you need to do 'Level 6' training. If you plan to stop at CILEX qualification you only need to complete 1 practice unit, 2 law units and both professional skills units. If you plan to go onto cross qualify as a solicitor you will need to undertake further law units, similar to the subject studied at part of a degree.

Completion of Level 6 will usually take 4 years part time, but the beauty of flexible part time study is that you can fit it around you and complete it sooner or take longer. I completed the requisite Level 6 qualifications for fellowship, plus the additional units required for cross qualification in 3 years. However, I would say this was not an easy task while working full time. I was eager to be qualified as soon as possible.

In addition to the academic training you must also complete 3 years of qualifying employment, and demonstrate, through the production of a portfolio, that you have met 8 competencies broken down into 27 learning outcomes. It sounds complicated, but the majority of it is straightforward and collated through your employment. Ultimately you already have the evidence there; the real challenge is collating it into one place. For example, to demonstrate communication skills you would submit a copy of an email you have sent to a client or a third party in the course of your employment and to demonstrate an evaluation of risks, costs and benefits you would provide an example of where you have completed such an analysis. Qualifying employment is usually undertaken while you are studying so they run in tandem.

To cross qualify as a solicitor and become regulated you will need to complete the LPC and Professional Skills Course. From starting the Level 3 to completing the LPC and becoming eligible for qualification it took me a total of 7 years.

The main advantage of qualifying via CILEX is that you can earn while you are learning. You have an income and can become qualified with no debt and learn invaluable commercial awareness from working within a law firm..."

FIRM-SPECIFIC LPCs

A number of Magic Circle (if you don't know what I mean by this – don't worry – it'll become clear later) and other large City firms currently have their own LPCs – where you'll meet other future trainees following a fast track programme at the same Law School (typically BPP Law School in London). The electives on such a programme will be specifically tailored to help prepare you for life in the City and in the firm of your choice. It'll also be a great opportunity to get to know your future colleagues!

ALL CHANGE PLEASE!

The above routes are the available ones at the time of going to press but not for long. The Solicitors Regulation Authority (our regulator and one of my clients) announced in Spring 2017 that the new Super Exam will be the pathway for making the grade by 2020.

The finer details are TBD but here's the latest insight from The Lawyer 2B magazine:

> *"In order to qualify as a solicitor, candidates will need to:*
>
> *•Have passed SQE stages 1 and 2 to demonstrate they have the right knowledge and skills*
>
> *•Have been awarded a degree or an equivalent qualification, or have gained equivalent experience*
>
> *•Have completed at least two years of qualifying legal work experience*

•Be of satisfactory character and suitability

As a result, the SRA will drop the requirements for all aspiring solicitors to study the Legal Practice Course (LPC) and for non-law graduates to take the Graduate Diploma in Law (GDL). This, says the SRA, eliminates the current problem of many would-be solicitors having to pay large up-front costs of up to £15,000 without a guarantee of a training contract or becoming a solicitor.

The first stage of the SQE will involve six functioning legal knowledge assessments and one practical legal skills assessment. The SRA anticipates this will be the cheaper part of the exam, and can be taken before the required period of work experience. It also anticipates that some universities will reshape their law degrees to incorporate teaching that will enable students to pass part one...

The second part of the SQE would be taken on the point of qualification and will involve two sessions of five practical legal skills assessments, which include client interviewing, advocacy and persuasive oral communication, case and matter analysis and legal research.

A period of work experience will also be required. This must total at least two years and could take the form of a traditional training contract, but could also take other forms. Work experience from up to four different organisations will be allowed to count towards the qualification requirement.

The current requirement for students to experience both a contentious and a non-contentious area of law during their period of work experience will also vanish, though the exam will test them on both.

Candidates that have already started a law degree, GDL or LPC by the time the super-exam is implemented in 2020 will have a choice of whether to follow the old route or to take the new SQE."

In short, WATCH THIS SPACE…

<u>ALL IMPORTANT TIMING</u>

Oh yes, if you're reading this because you're currently an undergraduate and either working through your options or you know what you want to do and are just trying to work out how to get it, you'll probably already be aware that the best time for applying to City firms and certain regional firms (who offer payment towards your CPE and/or LPC) is the penultimate year of your undergraduate degree. If the relevant firm runs vacation schemes (see Chapter 3) then this is also generally when you need to apply for these. If it's not clear from another firm's website when you need to apply – ask them. Their HR/ Grad Recruitment contacts will always be ready to help. They are looking for the best talent to join them after all!

I should also say – whenever you're picking this book up in life – it's never too late. Provided you're willing to be patient going through the post-graduate/ work-based motions/ discipline which is required to become a lawyer and assuming something resonates with you in this book – you'll have a story to tell: you just need to become a raconteur.

GOT IT? STILL WANT IT? LET'S PROCEED…

The Student Experience

I don't need to tell you how important University will be to the rest of your life and your career. If you're still an undergraduate or even a post-grad or you're doing your LPC or conversion course, make the most of every social and cultural experience that your institution has on offer – but don't forget to enjoy yourself!

What you do at University will be crucial to your Training Contract application. Your grades will obviously be a critical part of that. We'll discuss how to explain less than satisfactory grades later in the book. However, your other experiences – extra-curricular stuff – will be a massive part of your individual story in the application.

There are pretty obvious things you can do to get noticed. The President of a Law Society at a Russell Group University will probably have no end of suitors, but we can't all be him or her, and, frankly, most of you probably have no desire to be. But involvement in Societies is a great thing to put on your resume, whatever they might be. I set up a Buddhist Society at my University and acted as Treasurer. I was interested in meditation and attended temple with the Thai Society but I wanted to be part of something with a more specific focus on what I was interested in. There wasn't much of a budget involved in the role of Treasurer but we did need to organise and budget for certain social activities and manage charitable donations. Not a lot of work really, if I'm honest, but an interesting thing to add to the mix. It naturally led to questions at interview: how did you get interested in Buddhism? How did it impact your life? What did you do as treasurer?

I was also involved in the "Welsh Society" which was really a patriotic drinking club but, let's be honest, the trick is applying the right level of spin in terms of what you got out of such experiences to engage conversation without being entirely disingenuous. I was actually interviewed by a fellow Welshman in one interview and it gave me a useful "in" to talk about rugby and make a joke about the "objectives" of the Society. You might just strike it lucky in finding common ground with someone in Graduate Recruitment who might be reviewing your application or an interviewer like I did. They're looking for genuinely interesting and active people at the end of the day. You don't need to be in the AmDram club or Philosophical Society to fit that bill.

If you're sporty or artistic or musical and involved in such clubs in University, again, this is a great thing to shout about. The key, whatever it is that you enjoy doing, is to be able to link in their relevance to your decision to be a lawyer. Again, you could do a mind-map or something similar with key words to achieve this, e.g.:

- University Football Team → team player, sociable, driven

- Buddhist Society Founder and Treasurer → organised, passionate, focussed, interested in stress-handling techniques, mindfulness

- Welsh Society → patriotic (why not?) and passionate, sociable, and so on...

We'll talk about this in later Chapters but, suffice to say, get involved and get thinking. One common deficiency in a lot of applications is where people say (in a manner very similar to the annoying candidates on the Apprentice, often with very limited life experience or experience in business – rant over) "I'M REALLY DRIVEN, AND REALLY ENJOY PLAYING IN A TEAM, NOTHING STANDS IN MY WAY. I'M ALSO REALLY ARTICULATE AND ORGANISED AND ENJOY RUNNING PROJECTS". This is in total isolation and without any examples to evidence it. When you're telling your story about how your University life has shaped you and made you want and be ready for a career in the law, bear this in mind.

What you don't know won't help you...

I'm going to let you into a little secret.

Ssssshhhhhh....

don't tell anybody but: law/career fairs are not just about free bottle openers, sweets and key-rings. They're incredibly useful events in numerous ways.

I mentioned in the first chapter of this book that I had an encounter with a trainee solicitor at the firm where I spent the majority of my career, Baker McKenzie, which pretty much changed my life. She was a really interesting person and she at least appeared to love her job. But more than that, she seemed to take an interest in me when, not least because of my rather casual attire at the time (even more so than your average student if I'm honest), no one else really did. She was down to earth, she gave live and interesting examples of what she did every day (no doubt she sexed it up a bit), and she wore a huge smile on her face. Sold!

I don't recall her name. I wish I did because I'd actually quite like to thank her for her time 15 years ago and what it meant for my life between then and now. But I did note it at the time and I mentioned her and our useful discussion in my application form. I don't know what actual weight was given to that when it came to giving me a job but I like to think it might have been a "differentiating factor" which caught the eye. I don't think that many other people took that approach.

What I subsequently learned on joining the firm is that Law Fairs and Opening Evenings are not just a firm's opportunity to showcase their talent and what they can offer aspiring young lawyers. It's an opportunity for you to show your enthusiasm and to ask directed questions which (a) might help you decide whether the firm is the right one for you (or even if the law is the right path for you) and (b) might just get you your first contact with Graduate Recruitment decision-makers.

This needs some careful thought though. There is clearly a risk of being irritating if you don't get the balance right. Trust me, I know. People need their personal space after all! But a few carefully pitched questions at the firm attendees at these events can make a difference. Certainly, at my firm it was not uncommon for Graduate Recruitment to say to trainee/ associate attendees: did anyone stand out for you tonight? Did they ask any interesting questions? It may only be a toe-nail in the door but in a process of very fine margins, it can be the difference.

What do lawyers do?

If I was interviewing a candidate for a traineeship, this would be my first question. It's not a trick question, but it might feel like one if you haven't really thought about it. And it's almost criminal in my view for anyone to even think about approaching a training contract application without answering it themselves.

You may know first-hand what lawyers do. You may have carried out work experience, summer placements, or you may know a lawyer personally. If this is the case, include this in your mind-map. It may be that these experiences or the people you know have inspired you to become a lawyer yourself or you may want to be a lawyer in spite of certain experiences or people! It's all good stuff – it's all real – and so write it down!

On the other hand, you may not have studied or been studying law and you have no real idea what a lawyer does. Whether this is the case or not, I recommend you dwell on this question for a wee while. Challenge your assumptions. Dig deep:

- What is the difference between a solicitor and a barrister?
- Why do you want to be a solicitor?
- What type of solicitor do you want to be?
- What does a corporate lawyer do?
- What do you know about litigation?
- Describe a typical day in the life of a lawyer.
- What is the rule of law?
- What is the "business" of law?

You may be wondering: "how do I answer these questions?" There are a number of options. The starting point is often the internet:

- "Lawyer2Be" has some great information on this: http://l2b.thelawyer.com/careers/so-you-want-to-be-a-lawyer/134634.article

- The Law Society is also helpful: http://www.lawsociety.org.uk/law-careers/becoming-a-solicitor/

- As are industry web-sites such as RollonFriday: http://www.rollonfriday.com/

Speak to as many people as you can. If you can make a connection to a solicitor – high street firms will often be very happy to accommodate students on work experience. Alternatively, write to judges, court staff, get involved in your University Law Society – think outside the box. There are plenty of opportunities out there, many of which come out pretty well in the effort/reward stakes.

For me, failure to undertake this exercise is not an option. Otherwise attending a training contract interview where you might just get an offer which could change your life could be analogous to walking down the aisle with a blind date. Not only do you need to know this stuff to be believable and engaging at interview, you need to know it to make sure that you're travelling down a challenging path on an informed basis. It may or may not work in the long-term but you must try before you buy.

Find your inner narcissistic and tame it...!

As we progress in this book to talk about finding the right firm and applications and interviews, etc, one important thing to bear in mind is that you should not be afraid to blow your own trumpet. No one else will do it for you and everyone else will be doing it too.

That said, striking balances between confidence and arrogance, believability and bravado and humility and being underwhelming is a great art. Few achieve it on their first go. I once attended a training course designed around leadership and was asked the question: according to a survey of Chief Executives at the FTSE100 companies, what quality did these businessmen and businesswomen admire most about their colleagues and peers? Numerous answers flew around: "Confidence" "Intelligence" "Gravitas. The answer was, in fact, *calmness*. That's stuck with me ever since. It's the obvious choice really. When the pressure is on what everyone needs is a cool head to steady the ship. Someone with solutions, not problems – that's important for leaders and followers (and I certainly don't use the latter term in a derogatory way – being a key follower is as vital as being a leader).

Why is this relevant to you? Well, I think if you can bear this in mind in the application process and in interviews (indeed, in your entire career), you'll be halfway there. If you don't have this skill-set yet, recognising that and thinking about "how" you get it will serve you equally well. Graduate Recruitment and interviewers (lawyers and non-lawyers) will not be looking for the finished article. No one really is – even the most senior and respected lawyers – that's part of what makes them brilliant. But if you can talk to your strengths confidently and articulately describe what qualities you want to work on and why, you'll demonstrate a level of insight which will intrigue people involved in the applications process sufficiently to want to learn more about you.

CHAPTER 3
THE RIGHT LAW FIRM?

This question is inextricably linked to the question posed in the previous chapter: is the law right for you? In one sense, this is kind of like asking "is business right for you?" Or even "do you like music?" The topics are so wide-ranging that the answer goes far beyond a simple "yes" or "no".

Another common misconception is that all lawyers do the same thing or work the same way. They don't. They really don't. I know some really sophisticated corporate lawyers at top firms who have no idea what a commercial litigator does at a regional firm. Speaking to old school chums, when I say "I'm a solicitor" a common response is (assuming that I practise criminal law) "ohhh, how can you defend someone that you know is innocent?"

Amazing, but ignorance is not restricted to those outside the profession and ignorance is definitely not bliss. Look again at your mindmap. Does this give you some clues about the sort of lawyer you might want to be and/or the sort of firm you might want to work at? Don't panic. I'm not expecting you to have all the answers at this stage in your career. In fact, there is a risk that if you're TOO sure about the type of lawyer you want to be it can be off-putting or come across as narrow-minded. If you're interviewed by people not of the same TYPE as you aspire to, you might lose their interest before you've even begun.

I knew that I wanted to do something contentious. Intellectual property cases always sounded pretty interesting. I really liked medical ethics. I didn't know as a student that my path would lead me to a fair diet of commercial litigation and public law. If you're a law student, you're more likely to have a feel for what areas excite you. If you're not a law student, don't be afraid to look outside the box for inspiration to explain why you're considering a career in law. Are you attracted by the idea of being a technical whiz behind a corporate process, or do you enjoy debating and are intrigued by life in a court-room? Jot down some ideas and, if they're not already there, build them into your mindmap.

Your inspiration might be the media or television. It might be a general interest in business – law students, work experience students and summer interns (again, in my experience) often forget that lawyers are business people with as much of a focus on winning work and thinking about their position in the marketplace as they have on the law. It might be family or friends. It may even be as innocuous as a chance encounter with an inspiring young solicitor at a law fair who you thought was a really interesting and sold the work well(!) Some of you might be thinking "I just want to be rich". Personally I wouldn't open with that but I think there is a lot to be said for a bit of honesty especially when it's provided alongside a healthy serving of humility. In my training contract application I certainly focused on the importance I attached to being "upwardly mobile". Coming from a State school background (where careers advice largely centred around selling whatever GNVQ was in vogue that month), I attached great pride to attending a Russell Group University and wanted to have a career which would make my family (immediate and future – my children and my children's children) proud and secure them for life.

Once you have an idea of what sort of lawyer you want to be or think you might be well-suited to, this should give you a bit more of a steer in terms of which firm will suit you. Research on the firm is critical to a successful application – whether that's to a Magic Circle firm or a firm of high street solicitors or anything in between. "Magic Circle" by the way is not a reference to the world's premier magic society. It's a reference to the five 'leading' (British) law firms in the UK (by reference to metrics such as overall revenue and profits per equity partner) – they are: Allen & Overy, Clifford Chance, Freshfields Bruckhaus Deringer, Linklaters and Slaughter & May. There is also the "Sliver Circle" (a tier down in the same stakes but prestigious nonetheless) which includes: Herbert Smith Freehills, Ashursts, Berwin Leighton Paisner, Macfarlanes and Travers Smith. Collectively the "big boys" of British law firms in the UK.

Again, a really common error (but one which has been endorsed by a number of people I know in Graduate Recruitment and HR in law firms) is that people say "I'm great at this, I'm great at that..." OR "This firm is great at this, this firm is great at that" but the two aren't married together. I appreciate that this is not rocket science but, honestly, you'd be amazed at the **frequent lack of joining the two parts [I call this "mirror theory" and it's a theme I develop as we travel through the remainder of this book...]**

Your mindmap is probably already getting pretty busy but see if you can sprout out a few elements regarding the firm you're looking at. Mine (albeit with more than a pinch of hindsight – thinking about the two firms I've worked at) would look something like **Mindmaps #2a and #2b** in the Appendix

For me, working out the right firm or type of firm for you is made of the following core elements:

- What type of work do I want to do?

- What type of law is of most interest (non-lawyers, this will not mean a lot to you at this stage but you can be fairly generic – see below)?

- What type of working culture do I see myself being a part of?

- Where do I want to work (i.e. location in the UK or elsewhere)?

Let's take each of those in turn – for some of you, this might appear to be "teaching a grandmother to suck eggs" (LOVE that expression...). You may even be well-advanced down the process but I am of the firm belief that, even if you're drowning in books and web-pages providing a wealth of information on training contracts, it's often good to go back to basics and really interrogate your motives. If nothing else I find it helps: (i) you to come across as more genuine and believable in your application and (ii) it also, somewhat strangely, helps people to write more straightforwardly – because they're not over-thinking things.

What TYPE of work do I want to do?

The standard "holy trinity" of lawyers is: transactional, contentious and advisory.

Personally, I'm not a fan of this sort of categorisation because most transactional (i.e. generally corporate/ finance) lawyers will say that they are advisors on the law and business as well as being jolly good transactors. Equally, a traditional "advisory" lawyer – think pensions/ tax/ commercial/employment – will often dip their toes in the murky waters of litigation and provide a critical role in "corporate support" (i.e. advising their "transactional" colleagues about specific issues in a deal which are their "bag"). Litigators (I'm biased – we are of course THE BEST) are obviously primarily "contentious" types but we also pride ourselves on being problem solvers and being well-placed to advise on what to do before the proverbial hits in the fan. We'd also consider settlement agreements to be pretty "transactional" in character.

Criminal lawyers might do all three - arguably. I'm going out on a limb here but they'll be well-familiar with the workings of a court-room [CONTENTIOUS], will be best-placed to advise you on your options if you're ever arrested [GOD FORBID – ADVISORY] and you might need them to help you (figure of speech) to "do a deal" (i.e. a plea bargain) [I know it's a stretch – but TRANSACTIONAL?]

The point is: don't fall into the trap of thinking that knowing the trinity exists and writing about it at length will score you points. Really understanding how every lawyer should be skilled at all three is vital to the piece.

What AREAS of law interest you?

- Criminal?
- Civil?
- Commercial?
- Litigation?
- Corporate?
- Contract?
- Trusts?
- Property?

The list goes on. The wonder of the internet these days is that, if you don't know whether or not the above topics are interesting (particularly in you're a non-lawyer), there is a wealth of information out there to test the waters.

Ok, let's delve deeper. *Why do they interest you?*

- Criminal law: "it's fundamental to our way of life. The key tenet is ensuring justice..."

- Trusts: "It's arguably the greatest legacy England has given the world – the law of Trusts. It was developed as far back as the twelve century at the time of the crusades" [History Majors take note]
- Property: "I was fascinated by the impact of the Global Financial Crisis on the property market. How is often viewed in this country as one of the most basic requirements and desires of modern life – to own one's home. It touches on almost all areas of business from retail and the high street to farming and agriculture..." [Scientists/ agriculturalists/ economists]
- Litigation: "I have always enjoyed debating. At school I was part of a debating club where we considered issues as far ranging as "is force ever justified in achieving peace" to "an Englishman's home is his castle and God help he who seeks to knock down his walls – whether people should be allowed to strike down trespassers in their homes without fear of prosecution. I enjoy considering the elements of evidence which might put my side's best foot forward in a case but also playing devil's advocate and seeking to pre-empt my rival's arguments..."

If you're struggling to work this out, try this: think about what really interests you in life. Forget the law. Think hobbies, passions, TV shows, other entertainment, history, family connections –

anything. Try putting it into google or the search engine on Twitter with hashtags which might find you a link to the law. For example, #videogames #law (Intellectual Property Law?). Or #politics #law (a career in public and administrative law? Or human rights?). #TV #law (defamation?). #business #law (mergers and acquisitions?). The possibilities are pretty endless...

You must remember that, if we're talking the "holy trinity" of lawyer-types, different "transactional" types might deal in particular sectors (e.g. healthcare and pharmaceuticals, media, crowd-funding, energy, etc), just as a commercial litigator will deal with a variety of different disputes with a range of outcomes from multi-million dollar claims to reputation management, judicial review to investigations, arbitration to adjudication. Don't be fearful of the multitude of possibilities – embrace it and start to think about your place within it. You aren't expected to have all the answers now – far from it. Firms will be looking for candidates that are open-minded and after a varied career, but they're also looking for people who "get it" and have an embryonic view about what they might do with their life.

What type of CULTURE do you want to work in?

I'm going to lump this together with: **WHERE do you want to work?**

Because the answers to both are part of a recipe for where you see your future (short, medium and long-term). Some of you may have your whole lives mapped out and some may be totally freaked out by the question (as many of you will be – if you're in in your early twenties) as to what your long-term future looks like. There is no "right" answer here. I'm a big fan of the Everybody's Free (To Wear Sunscreen) song by Baz Luhrmann:

> *Don't feel guilty if you don't know what you want to do with your life.*
>
> *The most interesting people I know didn't know at 22 what they wanted to do with their lives*
>
> *Some of the most interesting 40-year-olds I know still don't*

Baby steps are usually best. Do you picture yourself in a big firm? A "corporate" environment? (This is in inverted commons because I don't even know what I mean by this. I'm sort of picturing something out of "Wolf of Wall Street" even though, having worked in the biggest law firm in the world I know it's nothing like this.) Do you want to work on "big ticket" deals or litigation (by "big ticket" I mean $$$$, not necessarily the importance of the issues)? Is firm prestige a big driver for you?

This may sound like an odd question but think about it: are you after a fairly 9-5 workload or are you content with (or do you even embrace) the prospect of working around the clock (from time to time)?

Do you want to be at a firm which is based within a fairly small community? At a small firm where you will be expected to take on and run cases very early on? Or do you like the idea of working in a mid-sized firm where there are sufficient resources to provide a well-structured training contract, with a reassuring number of trainees (so you don't end up embarrassingly introducing yourself to other trainees from the same firm at business events – I've seen it done many times)?

Do you want to be at a firm where pro bono work or Community activities are given high priority? Do you want to be part of a firm where social justice is at its heart?

Graduating the "where" to the same level as the "what", do you picture yourself in London? Or another major city in the UK? Perhaps you dream of working in another jurisdiction (in Europe or beyond), and/or you want to utilise your language skills?

These answers should be built into your mindmap.

So, what is the right firm for me?

People often reverse engineer this process, particularly law students. They like the 'sound' of a firm based on anecdotal evidence they hear around the law library or following the firm-sponsored presentation or law fair. Then they work out why that firm might want to hire them. In my experience, this is not a strategy which promotes longevity in life choices. Sure, write down the pointers you pick up from these experiences – you don't want to discount them because you listened to them for a reason but I would encourage you to think around these issues before committing yourself.

Once you have collated these thoughts, get researching. I've already mentioned rollonfriday.com. It has a page "Inside Info" which breaks down background info on the different City and regional firms. In places it could do with a bit of an update (the Baker McKenzie summary has not changed much since I applied for a training contract, although the firm itself has changed quite a bit) but it's a useful starter for ten. It also provides outline info on salaries and benefits. Legal Cheek's website is another great resource with stats on average office hours, salaries, diversity, trainee retention rates and minimum criteria for applications (which is picked up in the next Chapter). It also grades the firm, based on Insider Information, for all-important matters such as work/life balance, "partner approachability", training, peer support, quality of work and chances of international secondments.

"Chambers and Partners" and "The Legal500" are other useful resources. They will help you narrow down firms by specialist area and location. They will also give you examples of deals and cases different firms have worked on around that time which will be useful fodder for applications and interview answers. It will provide gold on your interviewers when you get there – flattery (delicately deployed) is a pretty powerful tool!

Having defined the above parameters, you also can't beat a bit of searching via search engines but also via social media. More and more firms are using Twitter, LinkedIn, HuffPost, etc and "Thought Leadership" at innovate firms (ahem, like my own) and thinking about how to drive internet traffic to their web pages using #hashtags. If you have a series of interest areas in your mindmap, find out who's tweeting about them.

Use these mechanisms to initially cast your net pretty widely and then narrow it down until a manageable number and then STICK.

Work experience and vacation schemes

You can't beat actually stepping through the doors of a firm in order to understand what type of lawyer you want to be at what type of firm. The best way to do that is either to talk your way into doing some free work experience - most small to mid-sized firms will bite your hand off at coming to their office and helping them out for a couple of weeks. Adding a firm's name to your CV – even for a short stint may be the difference to getting the ultimate job.

The larger firms have vacation scheme programmes which are widely recognised as being like 'gold dust' – firms generally take fewer "vaccies" than the size of their annual trainee intakes. These are brilliant gigs if you can get them for several reasons:

Firstly, of course they're an opportunity to experience first-hand what it is to be a trainee in a law firm. You'll be mentored by those already doing the job. An opportunity to ask them questions, watch them work, and try the trainee suit on for yourself.

Second, they'll be an invaluable opportunity to show the firm what you can do. I can't emphasise that enough. I have been surprised in the past about how some 'vaccies' have approached the task with nonchalance and even arrogance; not respecting the gift they've been given. I was fortunate enough to have participated in three vacation schemes in 2003

– at Baker McKenzie, Allen & Overy and Herbert Smith. Each one an incredible opportunity and brilliant experience: experiencing different departments, different lawyers' styles and corporate cultures. I threw myself into absolutely every task I was given from photocopying to researching difficult legal questions; writing articles and drafting presentations to attending meetings and taking notes. I was even fortunate enough to savour a courtroom drama or two.

During one scheme I attended a huge case in the High Court between Formula One giants Eddie Jordan and Vodafone. It gave me a taste for a litigator's life that I'll never forget. I remember I had a stinking cold at the time and was coughing and spluttering throughout the sessions. So much so I even caught the eye of Mr Jordan who gave me a wink when I suffered a coughing fit at the back of the courtroom. Even though I felt like hell I still made a point to ask pointed questions of the trainees and associates I attended with, offered to pick them up drinks and snacks, and generally make myself a useful resource.

In another scheme the 'vaccies' were pitted against one another in a "balloon debate". We each drew a celebrity out of a hat and had to say in each round why our celebrity should be saved from being thrown out of the hot air balloon. I didn't draw the best card – Gordon Ramsay at the height of his swearing, ranting fame but I won the whole contest – beating Joan of Arc in the finale! I remember Joan of Arc (who by this point was running out of ideas) talking about God and faith – a lot. I was also running low on inspiration – using my cooking for my fellow balloon mates to the nth degree – and simply responded "well, if God is on your side, you stand a better chance being chucked out of this balloon than me!" It did the trick. Bottle of champagne in the bag – but, more importantly, it got me noticed.

Third, they're a great opportunity to make new friends and contacts – to socialise (in a responsible way, of course – even though there is generally a free bar) and to get decision makers one on one. I appreciate that sounds a little creepy and have first-hand experience of 'vaccies' being over-keen. That might fly in the face of the theme here but there is a balance. Asking questions and listening to the answers. Being human and interesting and excitable but not puppy-dog like – got it?

I remember on my Baker McKenzie vacation scheme getting into a conversation with a female partner and asking her questions about her latest venture – into motherhood(!). I asked her how she managed to balance being a partner at a global law firm with being a mum. I'll never forget her answer. She told me she thought she did two jobs badly: she wasn't a good enough partner for the firm or mother to her son. That really shook me but her honesty was so refreshing it was one of the reasons I chose to join Baker McKenzie. I wanted a firm where I could be vulnerable and unsure – where I could ask the "stupid" questions and not be judged for it and Baker McKenzie was it.

Finally, vacation schemes usually pay a decent salary for the 2 or 3 weeks work. Certainly, the most money I'd had at the time by some distance – which gave me the necessary funds for other adventures before I started the world of work.

In short, I highly recommend that you look into what firms do vacation schemes and think about applying for one as a precursor to an application for a training contract. Approach a vacation scheme application in the same way you would a training contract application…READ ON

CHAPTER 4
THE APPLICATION

Now, I hope you haven't skipped straight to this Chapter. The other Chapters set the scene for this nail-biter and I would advise that you read the joke before the punchline…!

RE-CAP/ MIRROR THEORY

OK, so we've talked about our "stories". How we got to this point. Why we want to go for this job. You should by now have quite a developed mindmap as to why you're going to piece together a compelling application to whichever firm/s you've decided are the right fit for you. You've found your inner narcissist and you've tamed him/ her.

The next skill or lesson to master (as prefaced in the previous Chapter) is what I call **"MIRROR THEORY"**. Everything you do from this point forward is about you and about the firm/s you're applying to. That might sound obvious but the mastery in the trick is in the marriage of the two. If you flick ahead to the next Chapter, we build on mirror theory in the interview process – every question you're asked, every pathway you go down -

***it's not about the "You" or the "Me" –
it's about the "Us"***

Imagine that you're about to embark on a very professional and civilised courtship. You have to explain why you and the firm/s make the perfect couple.

It's very easy to fall into the trap of talking yourself up but forgetting about why your brilliance is relevant to a firm already jam-packed with brilliant people. Equally, many people drool over a firm and are quite happy to explain why the job is the dream job – but losing sight of why you are right for it. THE KEY IS REMEMBERING THAT:

IF YOU'RE ASKED A QUESTION ABOUT YOU – MAKE IT AS MUCH ABOUT THE FIRM AND

IF YOU'RE ASKED A QUESTION ABOUT THE FIRM – MAKE IT AS MUCH ABOUT YOU

THIS IS NOT AN EASY TRICK AND REQUIRES PRACTICE

YOUR PREFERRED FIRM/S BRAND/S

Before you work out what you want to say about you – whether in a CV or in an application – add a branch to your mindmap about the BRAND, ETHOS OR CORE VALUES of the firm you're applying to. It'll give you the key or buzz words which should permeate this entire process.

This is a little known 'trick' which will really make you stand out. When I was at Baker McKenzie, its core value was "fluency". Being one of the biggest firms in the world, with a multitude of offices across an ever-growing number of jurisdictions, you can see why that would make sense. The message was: no matter what office you contact, whatever the size of the case or deal, you would get the same, high quality service across the world.

At Capital we have five core values which we're reminded of on our internal systems every day: approachability, integrity, boldness, excellence and clarity.

Examples of other firms, e.g. Eversheds' values are:

- Looking after our clients' interests as though they are our own

- Being straightforward, open and honest

- Putting the firm's interests ahead of individual agendas
- Treating everyone with respect, fairness and courtesy
- Being accountable for our clients and colleagues
- Striving for continuous improvement

Clifford Chance refer to elements of CC "DNA" which includes:

- Exceeding clients' expectations
- Local excellence, global standards
- An ambition for success
- Investing in talent
- An adaptable and approachable team
- Thinking ahead
- Strength through diversity
- Community

And, personal favourite of mine, Fieldfisher say on their site: "Characters welcome, don't leave your personality at home…"

Now think about how the firm's brand connects with your own brand. This is the first layer of mirror theory for the purpose of your application…

YOUR PERSONAL BRAND

YES, YOU'RE A BRAND: One which has been evolving throughout your life and will continue to evolve in your career.

What's my personal brand? As it stands, I'd say I'm:

CREATIVE, EMPATHETIC AND CREDIBLE WITH A FIRST CLASS LEGAL PEDIGREE

That's not easy for me to say – AHEM – but I said it!

I'll add that to **Mindmap #3** in the Appendix…

How did I come up with this? Well, it's what I feel about myself, it's what others have said to me and what I hope others think about me too. It's aspirational but I wouldn't write it if I didn't believe it was also accurate. I have worked at the biggest and best, I have found my creative edge especially since I've been at the fantastic, growing firm where I am now and, sometimes, I'm too honest for my own good but I believe that, to be credible and strong, you need to be true to yourself.

How does that connect with my firm's values? Well, pretty well actually. The creativity is important to a firm which focusses so obviously on innovative and BOLD solutions. I once put a comic strip together as part of a pitch. Fortunately, it was well-received!

Empathy? Well, when CORE VALUES include INTERGRITY AND APPROACHABLITY empathy is a pretty key characteristic in my book. As demonstrated by the very fact that I've written this book, I feel I have something to offer junior lawyers. One of the best parts of my job is helping others build the careers they want.

There are lots of useful online resources about building and leveraging your personal brand. Personal favourites of mine? #AskGaryVee is a great speaker on this topic. I have to shout out to my compatriot Aimee Bateman – founder of great website CareerCake which includes a fantastic talk on the topic. You'll find some real gems talking about this stuff online. One of my favourite sources of inspiration – indeed, an inspiration in writing this book, is/ are "TEDTalks" – a series of inspired talks about all sorts of topics. They're short and sweet and insightful. I generally find that there are one or two tit-bits to take into my own life and professional career in every one that I watch. They're a theme I pick up in the next Chapter as well. TED Talks are generally available on YouTube and there's a dedicated App too. Check it out…

One great example is Rob Brown's humbling talk "The Personal Brand of you" from a TEDx convention in Nottingham a few years ago. In the modern world, it's absolutely imperative that you understand this art, hone it for your application and evolve your personal brand throughout your career. It's what'll get you noticed

SO HOW WOULD OTHERS DESCRIBE YOU (IN A GOOD WAY OF COURSE – WE ALL HAVE OUR LESS BRILLIANT ATTRIBUTES AS WELL!) IF YOU WERE NOT IN THE ROOM?

WRITE DOWN THE KEY WORDS AND THEN –

CONNECT THE DOTS * * * * * * * * * * * *

HOW DO THE TWO CONNECT TOGETHER?

Where are the connections and points of difference?

How is each of them evidence-based? What do I mean by this? Well, you don't want to say "I'm articulate, confident and a team-player…and so that fits well with your brand because you're also about team-work and standing out" because those words are empty. Anyone can say them. It's better to say something like:

> *I have discussed your firm's values with trainee solicitors at law fairs and with Graduate Recruitment at talks at my University. They've all been very approachable, articulate and wax lyrical about the quality of work and people at the*

firm. They explained how your key brand message is commerciality: why write 10 sentences if two will do? It's clear that you seek to understand the individual requirements of your clients, get to know the key decision-makers and tailor your approach. A great example of this was the recent deal involving company X and Y picked up in The Lawyer earlier this year.

I'm a big believer in being brief: cutting to the chase and tailoring my pointed message to the audience. As my University Lacrosse team Captain I have to work out how to help my team (and the different approaches of the individuals within it) tick and decide strategy under pressure.

My Creative Writing Major may, you might think, encourage longer form prose but – on the contrary – if you can't grab your reader's eye quickly and keep their attention they'll soon put your work down.

The "mirror theory" here is subtle. It isn't: "we're a perfect match because…" or "you're this and I'm that…" It flows from one message to the next.

The best way to achieve this sort of flow is to rely on your mindmap to do the work for you. Develop your brand – note those of your targets – illustrate the gaps with examples from firm news to your own life events, choices, hobbies and strengths. Write to sell.

Imagine being a Grad Recruitment professional: having to wade through tens, hundreds – even thousands of applications. You need to stand out by telling the most compelling story.

INTERVIEW NOTES

I may have laboured mirror theory a bit above but, for me, it's almost criminal to forget it in any job application – let alone one in such a competitive field.

I have read other books on this topic which give you example Q and As but this doesn't, in my humble opinion, reflect reality. The questions between applications/ firms will vary massively. There is always the temptation to lift wording direct from a book and try to make it your own but this isn't genuine and - at best – risks losing your originality and – at worst – risks plagiarism. I believe you can adapt this theory and tailor it to any application.

I also recommend that, before you start making applications, you read the next Chapter "The Interview". Your application is not just your best foot forward on paper; it should be your interview notes as well. If HR/ the reviewing lawyer likes the cut of your jib, they'll want to test it out in person too. But if you're inconsistent with how you describe yourself on paper, they'll think you disingenuous.

Being a good lawyer – hell, being a good professional – is about ambition and commitment but also about consistency in output and learning from successes and mistakes alike. It's a constant evolution and the application and interview process are the start of your evolution – treat them with respect and – if you believe in them – others will buy it too.

NOW THE "BORING" STUFF!

Minimum criteria

This is a tough business and training contracts are competitive. Some firms have minimum criteria: As and Bs at A Level, 2.1 degree (or predicted degrees)

If you don't have these credentials then you'll need to sharpen your focus. Be honest with yourself. If you're predicted a 2:2 then the very top London law firms may not be the place for you (although this might well depend on how compelling the rest of your story is). Certainly though there's no reason why a great regional or boutique City firm can't be home.

In this case, you'll need to explain why you haven't been top of the class in a way which is reflective, honest and real. Turn a negative into an aspirational positive. Say what you do best. It might be that you don't tick every box in an exam but you know people and the way they work. You may have excellent extra-curriculars. Maybe you even suffered a life event which shaped your path in a way you didn't expect. Make your explanation for how you have performed stand out for all the right reasons.

The important thing is not to be an ostrich: don't put your head in the sand. Front up and show your ambition in the process.

Qualities on paper

It's pretty tough to answer this question because no one firm (or, indeed, individuals within it) are looking for any one type of person: where's the fun in that?

That said; the following skills/ qualities can't hurt!

Motivated	Tell a personal story as to why you're motivated to this job
Perhaps how you've overcome adversity and it's made you a better person for it
As with all of these, don't just say you're motivated – prove that you are
You'll need this to survive a career in law – it's a tough

	enough job for those that are committed and motivated – I can't imagine what it's like if you're not
Team player	Team sports are great Academic clubs as well If you've already ventured into the world of work or business – fantastic. You may have had to work with people who are very different to you – how did you overcome these differences? Get out there and meet people and talk about your interactions
Articulate	Again, public speaking, debating, mooting – tick tick tick But perhaps you're more of an articulate writer: theorist, science lover or poet How do you communicate with the world?
"Transferable skills"	If you've had a job – any job – it will have helped develop skill sets which ordinary academics won't. Often you'll have experienced what good customer service means and that will be golden for tackling lawyer/ client relations. If what you've done is more production line – that, in my

	experience, requires patience, attention to detail, etc
	There is a spin on any work experience – just get some!
	The real world gives you a real story – see below

Be original

I often cringe when I look at law firm websites and see the same old slogans and buzz phrases. They do exactly what I've suggested in this book you shouldn't. Say what they think they are without evidencing it. It's clear that what they've done is get some whizzy PR guru in to manifest a new brand and image without that whizzy PR guru having any experience of what any law firm does/ what's different about the firm they're advising.

One of the most common offenders are firms which describe themselves as "innovative" without showing a crumb of originality or different products or offerings. "Innovation" has been a buzz word in the profession for a fair while now – long enough, in fact, that using it is no longer hip. At the time of writing (I say that because the next fad – even in law firms – is always around the corner) the new discussion point is what it means to be "Disruptive"…

disruptive

causing or tending to cause disruption.

"disruptive pupils"

synonyms: troublemaking, troublesome, unruly, rowdy, disorderly, undisciplined, attention-seeking, riotous, wild, turbulent; More

unmanageable, uncontrollable, out of control/hand, unrestrained, obstreperous, truculent, fractious, divisive;

badly behaved, misbehaving, errant, uncooperative, rebellious;

disturbing, distracting, unsettling, upsetting, noisy, raucous;

formalrefractory

"a very disruptive child"

antonyms: well behaved, manageable

innovative or groundbreaking.

"breaking a disruptive technology into the market is never easy"

> *synonyms: innovative, inventive, ingenious, original, innovatory, innovational, new, novel, fresh, unconventional, unorthodox, off-centre, unusual, unfamiliar, unprecedented, avant-garde, experimental*

The "Disruptive GC" movement is a great example of this. They're breaking with traditional client/lawyer relationships and demanding more from their external advisers.

Innovation/ disruption/ originality come in all shapes and sizes. How are you different? How are you interesting? What have you done which makes you stand out from the crowd?

In my case it was probably wearing my heart on my sleeve. I came from a working-class family, a pretty quiet and uneventful town and went to the local comprehensive. I had a good childhood. I wanted for nothing. My mum and dad pretty much pushed their own desires and dreams to one side to make sure me and my sister had all the support we needed to achieve our dreams. I have family members who have suffered with mental health problems.

I wanted to leave my home town. I wanted the bright lights of the City. I wanted to be as big a success as I could possibly be in the only way I knew how – being the smartest, most dedicated lawyer any law firm would wish to have on its books.

[I appreciate it's not quite as sexy as a rock star story but it's not bad in my book...]

I made this point in my applications. I'm not going to say it will work for everyone but it worked for me. Most lawyers don't show vulnerability. I think you need to know your own potential limitations in order to work out how you tackle or avoid them and prosper.

Compassion

The same goes for compassion but there is an added dimension here. Corporate Social Responsibility (CSR)/ Working Responsible is a critical part of most commercial law firms make-ups these days. Most firms will have a CSR policy or programme. Some even have CSR professionals.

What can you find out about your target firm's CSR objectives? How do they approach the question of diversity amongst their workforce? What sort of *pro bono* (free legal work) work do they do? Are they active in their community (if so, how so?)? Do they have chosen charities they raise money for during the year? Do they help local businesses/ start-ups with initial legal work in some sort of preferential rate/ free arrangement? Do they steer away from working for clients in 'unethical' businesses (e.g. vulture funds)?

If the firm/s you're looking at do it – they'll probably shout about it quite loudly.

What do you do in this area? What charities are you close to? How have you given up your time to help others? How do you value your community?

This, in my experience, is an often neglected area of applications. People think "business, business, business" and forget about COMMUNITY.

"Commercial awareness"

I've never really liked this buzz phrase. All too often in business people stick two words together to make a 'thing' which then reverberates around the industry even though few really understand what it means. I first heard about "commercial awareness" when I was preparing for my training contract interviews. I was told by my peers that it was a critical part of an application process for a commercial law firm. The problem was that no one could explain to me what it was or 'where to get it'.

In a nutshell, it's the ability to understand the business world in a non-academic way. The reality is that many of you just won't have had the opportunity to delve into the business world in a natural way: unless you're a seasoned entrepreneur or have a family member who is and you've grown up watching them in action and asking them questions. I certainly didn't understand it when I was 20 years old and thinking about how to impress a forty-something partner in a commercial firm. A forty-something partner who can smell B.S. a mile off.

So, what did I do? Well, firstly I didn't panic because no-one is the complete package when they're applying for a job like this. Secondly, I came up with a plan which I thought would be enough to show I was taking this seriously without being something I wasn't. I bought a few copies of the Financial Times, looked for articles which interested me. To be honest, most of the articles didn't interest me (some felt like I was reading a foreign language), but there was always a 'hook' to certain stories which connected to my values, hobbies or interests.

For example, as a sport lover, there were some interesting stories about the financial elements of summer transfer dealings; maybe a story about something culturally engaging like the arts or music; or, more often when I've picked up the orange broadsheet lately, it's something about a tech business with a whizzy new idea or invention. Even in those cases, more often than not I needed google to look up certain business words but at least I had the incentive to get the translation.

Once I'd collected a few articles, I stuck them into a scrapbook and learned them 'off pat'. Where the opportunity arose or where it was relevant to the autobiographical sections of the application process, I weaved them in. When I got interviews in the bag I supplemented my scrapbook with news items about the firm/s, relevant deals and cases and drew out questions for the interviewer/s about the same. This 'trick' isn't for everyone and the key is to make it your own. The key to this whole process is to be organic. Be you. But to be the BEST version of you. ADAPT it to make it work FOR YOU...

The real world gives you a real story

I have met a lot of people from different walks of life in this line of business.

I've met people who have said to me "do you know what? I don't need this hassle....I made $35m selling my business...£8m is nothing to me..."

I've worked with charities which help terminally ill people, people on death row, and the poorest people in the third world.

Outside of work I have friends who have earned 7 figures in a year, or have had thousands and thousands from the bank of mum and dad, and others who can't afford to pay their rent.

People who are really like me and those that I don't get or just don't get me,

But what do they all have in common? They all – every single one of them – has at least one story about their live/s or experiences which is compelling and which should be shared. You need to find yours.

CURRICIULUM VITAE

Some firms will ask you for a CV or resume instead of an application. In this case, keep it super simple:

NAME/ CONTACT

PERSONAL STATEMENT

Keep it very brief and be original – catch the eye

EDUCATION

An overview of your qualifications – don't list every subject you've ever studied although some firms might require a breakdown of the subjects you've covered in your undergraduate degree and your marks (especially if you're studying Law)

WORK EXPERIENCE

Again, brief is the word. Name of employer, dates you worked there and a sentence or two maximum on your responsibilities

OTHER SKILLS, EXPERIENCE & INTERESTS

Make sure it is interesting and relevant and – again, brief

References available on request

Depending upon the feel you have for the firm, you could make it a bit more interesting – even tailor it to them using the above guidance. Just make sure that, whatever you say, it's evidence-based throughout.

Finally, no CV should ever and I mean EVER be more than 2 pages long. I don't care if you're fresh out of school or a CEO at a Fortune 500 company with 40 years' experience. It should never ever be more than two pages. It's an insight into what makes you great; not an autobiography.

KEY RULES

Plain English

Don't swallow a thesaurus. Use plain English.

Make your application easily digestible and memorable for all the right reasons. This won't be as easy as it sounds because generally in University you're rewarded for writing in an academic way.

It's one of the first things I learned as a trainee at Baker McKenzie. As far as possible – write like you speak. Think about your audience. Write it down and then fold it away before submitting it and pick it up a day or two later. How does it read now?

Spelling and grammar

It's so easy to ruin a great application with poor attention to detail in terms of spelling and grammar. These days more than ever - you have computerised spell-checks and apps such as "Grammarly" at your fingertips.

HOW MANY APPLICATIONS?

I'm often asked this and you won't be surprised to hear that there is no right answer. I made around 8 applications; I had 5 offers of interviews; I attended 4 (politely declined another) and got 3 vacation schemes and 3 training contract offers. There is always a dash of luck in this process but mostly it's hard graft.

In short, do enough applications to give yourself the best chance of getting interviews but only as many as you're genuinely able to service in a bespoke and compelling way. Do lots of research into the firms which come up on your hit list and think about why you'd be the right fit for them. It's much better to do three compelling and well-engineered applications than 30 which are rushed out without careful thought. As a general rule of thumb though, you should (if you want to succeed in this business) have enough stamina to do 5-10.

SOCIAL MEDIA

Make your "application profile" consistent with your social media one. Don't abuse platforms such as Twitter and Facebook. These days HR departments are as likely to check your social media presence as they are your references. If you aren't generally very social media aware – become it. Don't use foul language. Try to limit the number of drunken photographs. It's been around long enough so that we all have some things on social media we're not so proud of – try and manage this if you can.

Think about other platforms which you should be on if you're not already. LinkedIn is a classic example. When your CV is ready (or you have enough golden nuggets from the application process), get it online and start connecting. You'll need this to do business when you get to work and so it can't hurt to get on it now…

CHAPTER 5
THE INTERVIEW

Congratulations! If you're reading this chapter in preparation for an interview – well done *[or you've just heeded my advice and are reading these in conjunction with Chapter 4 – either way, hurrah!]*!

You've done brilliantly to get this far and what happens next is the easy part (honestly!)…You've already been narrowed down to a select few and you're in the running. I still remember receiving interview letters (and the rejections). It was a rollercoaster of emotions: elation, pride, determination, nerves, and trepidation. It's probably all starting to feel a bit real now…

Well, you've already gone your mindmaps and a considered application to get you ready with the right content for answering questions at interview but, before we re-visit that, let's think about what other things you might do to get you in THE ZONE.

GETTING INTO THE "INTERVIEW STATE"

(My definition) The state of preparedness for an interview (or similar, typically stress-inducing experience) so that you're sitting in that waiting room feeling as though the information you need to process and divulge is ready and organised, you're feeling fit and mentally in check, and you're looking the part.

There are three critical pieces to this puzzle: stress management, body language and verbal techniques, and preparation.

Stress Management

There are some amazing books and studies out there on each of these puzzle pieces. Three examples I've recently enjoyed under this heading are: two TED talks – one by Dr Daniel Levitin (neuroscientist, musician and author) and another by Dr Kelly McGonigal (a health psychologist and lecturer at Stanford University); and the book Bounce: the Myth of Talent and the Power of Practice by Matthew Syed (a British table tennis Olympian and author). I recommend you check these out.

Kelly McGonigal's talk is one of the most watched TED talks of all time. Fantastically titled, "How to make stress your friend", McGonigal's talk shows just how it is done. She explains how throughout her career she has always held stress out as the enemy – responsible for physical ailments ranging from the common cold to heart disease. But then she came across a study which made her change her entire outlook. The study, published in 2011, was conducted by researchers at the University of Wisconsin-Madison who asked around 30,000 people to rate their level of stress over the past year AS WELL AS how much they believed this stress influenced their health — a little, a moderate amount or a lot. Over the next eight years, public death records were used to record the passing of any subjects.

The Results? Well, people who reported having high levels of stress had a whopping 43% increased risk of death BUT ONLY where those people BELIEVED that stress had a negative impact on their health. The same did not apply to those who didn't have this perception. IN FACT, those that experienced a lot of stress BUT DID NOT PERCEIVE its effects as NEGATIVE were amongst the least likely to die as compared to all other participants in the study (including people who had relatively little stress).

And so, stress is not bad for your health: how you feel about it may or may not be…

How is this explained? Well, those people in this category of "least likely" actually USED STRESS POSITIVELY TO PREPARE themselves for stressful situations or episodes in their lives. We normally view physical stress responses (heart pounding, breathing more quickly, perspiration) as "signs of anxiety or that we're not coping" but what if we used them as signs that you're "ENERGISED and preparing you to meet this challenge"?

This, McGonigal cross-refers in her TED Talk, was demonstrated in a Harvard University "Social Stress Test" (another one published in 2011). In this study, the participants were required to submit to a simulated interview situation, in which they performed a 5-minute presentation while two evaluators provided negative feedback. After giving the presentation, participants were required to complete a series of analytical questions. Before the interview, one group was told that stress was not harmful and that it would actually help them perform the presentation (the heart pounding will prepare you for action, the quickened breathing is more oxygen going to your brain, etc). The "control group" weren't given any instructions. The mental and physical responses of both groups were assessed after the interview.

One of the most interesting results from the test group was in their physical response to the stress.

One effect of stress is that your blood vessels restrict – this is a potentially dangerous and is linked with cardiovascular problems. This was the case for the "harmful stress" group. But the control group's response was fascinating. Looking at their blood vessels – they stayed relaxed. The picture of their vessels were more open, allowing blood to flow – the image actually looked a lot more like what your vessels look like in moments of joy.

This is why McGonigal urges you to make stress your friend. This idea is not one which is necessarily instantly received and incorporated into one's mental toolkit but it is one to think about. Use the stress you feel and understand that it's there to make you better, to raise your performance and you should – with some practice (by all means – practise in front your friends, family, lecturers) – help you 'ride the wave'.

Cognitive psychologist and neuroscientist Dr Levitin's ideas are, in my view (although the scientists may disagree) essentially based on the same principles. He talks about the "pre mortem" of a potentially stressful situation. You've all heard of a post-mortem, right? Well a pre-mortem involves walking your way through a potentially stressful situation, considering what might 'go wrong', and working through solutions or logical, prepared reactions to those 'problems' arising. Dr Levitin talks about how, in a stressful situation, our minds fog up and we can't think as rationally in terms of how to resolve situations as if we had done them in a neutral, un-stressful environment in advance. You might say that this flies in the face of McGonigal's conclusions because she talks about how to 'use' stress.

In my view, both of them are right and there is no contradiction. The point is, as more particularly detailed below, you can both prepare for various outcomes whilst also allowing your body to use its natural, hormonal reactions to put forward the best version of you when stressful moments arise.

Body Language and verbal techniques

Body language in interview situations has been a controversial topic in recent years. The most talked about body language theory in psychology and neuroscience circles has been the "POWER POSE" - standing in a posture of confidence, even when we don't feel confident:

There is a lot of research in support of the conclusion doing a POWER POSE shortly before a situation like a job interview can affect testosterone and cortisol levels in the brain – preparing you for the challenge and even improving your prospects of success. Cuddy's former research partners have since doubted the original research giving force to the theory. Personally, I'm with Cuddy. Having been through this process in recent years when I left a job of nearly a decade to take on a new challenge – in circumstances where, perhaps, my confidence was at an all-time low because I'd barely returned from maternity leave and hadn't found my 'groove' yet, and I hadn't had a proper interview in 12 or 13 years, it really worked.

I had two interviews. One for the firm I currently work in and another with Eversheds. Before both interviews I went to ladies bathroom, waited until I was pretty sure that no one was in the communal area, and looked in the mirror, took in a couple of deep and slow breaths in and out, and held my arms aloft for a couple of minutes. Risky strategy when anyone could have walked in at any moment but that 'danger' heightened my oxytocin levels further and I felt really good. I was *prepared*, I was ready, I believed in myself.

I got two job offers.

You can take or leave the POWER POSE because you've got to do what's right for you, but I certainly recommend you watch Cuddy's TED talk and see whether it might work for you.

The other important aspect is body language during the interview. This will be different for everybody. You will each have your own mannerisms and it's important you're true to who you are – but we can all work on being the best versions of ourselves. This isn't rocket science. Respectfully, it's quite simple.

Generally, the best form of handshake when you walk in the room is a firm but relaxed one. Don't squeeze their hand too hard but avoid being 'limp' at all costs. If you're prone to sweating, wash and dry your hands immediately before and try to warm them up if you can, e.g. under a hand-dryer in a bathroom. If your hands feel cold it can sometimes be a bit off-putting and if you're being interviewed in winter it smacks of "I've just walked in from off the street and haven't really thought about this at all". Practice your handshake. It might sound trivial but your initial handshake, your first connection into your interviewer(s) eyes, and the first words you say will set the tone for the rest of the interview.

So what do you say? Personally, I'd keep it simple – always use their first names (unless you've been given the heads up that they're overly formal – very few people are in my experience) confidently and say "Good to meet you X, I'm Y". Typically there may be some initial small talk. Us Brits love a good chat about the weather. Be ready for that but don't force it. I often like a little anecdote or two being exchanged. It shows the interviewee is relaxed, but keep it brief: you're here to do a job.

Make sure you're sitting comfortably. Crossed legs is fine provided your upper body is open. Allow yourself to breathe. Use your hands to express yourself if it feels natural but don't overdo it. If there is more than one interviewer make sure you make eye contact with all of them but don't be afraid to primarily address a question one person has raised to them, keeping the others involved and inviting their non-verbal feedback, returning to the person who asked the question when you finished. Sit upright. Avoid leaning one way or another. And, most importantly, SMILE. If you're using McGonigal's techniques you should, bizarre as this might sound, enjoy it.

If you're tasked with giving a presentation as part of your interview (you might even be given a case study before the interview starts) I'd recommend you take cue cards with you. Rustling paper is a no-no. Having cue cards to write your answers on when you read the case study will show the level of preparation and initiative for a future trainee solicitor! And if the preparation is pre-prepared the familiarity of the cue cards (and your presentation – well- but not over-rehearsed) will allow you to get the tone, pace and pitch perfect! Importantly, don't be a slave to any notes prepared in advance of the interview. You must engage your audience. This will show confidence (even if you don't feel it) and keep the interviewer/s interest.

Scope out the room to see whether it's best to stand or sit for a presentation: standing is often better because it shows you're quite happy and confident to stand when others are sitting but, in my view, sitting when you might be expected to stand can send the same message. I don't do too many client meetings standing. You need to be able to be understood and give an air of confidence when sitting too. If it feels right, ask the interviewer what they would prefer you to do. If you do stand though make sure you do so with your legs a short distance apart (crossed legs are a no-no here, as is rocking) and stand up straight (get air into your lungs). Use your arms as you would if you were sitting. Your hands and arms can be expressive and powerful but don't overdo it. I recommend watching how politicians do it in the House of Commons. Some do it better than others. The likes of David Cameron and Tony Blair were masters (at this, at least!). Barack Obama is another fantastic orator.

What about VERBAL TECHNIQUES?

Sorry – another TED Talk is crucial here. Watch Julian Treasure "Master of Sound" in action in "How to speak so that people want to listen…" In fact, watch any number of TED talks and you'll see great orators at work. They're all different: as will be the (hopefully many!) readers of this book. I think Julian's "7 deadly sins of speaking" are to be Treasure-d (my interpretation of each of them is below):

AVOID

GOSSIP – if you want to be taken seriously, be factual, not facetious

JUDGING – BE OPEN-MINDED AND FAIR

Negativity – positivity is engaging and inspiring, this quite the opposite

Complaining — you don't want to be remembered for the wrong reasons. Treasure says "misery is viral"

Excuses - not to be confused with explanations (see Applications chapter)

EXAGGERATION OR EVEN LYING – just don't do it. As lawyers, it's a fundamental part of our ethical code

Dogmatism – don't conflate fact and opinion – be clear about which you're stating or expressing

Ok, so those are the don'ts, but what about the things you should be doing? Treasure again has a theory – one which I ascribe to – **HAIL**. That is:

Honesty. Skilled interviewers will catch you out if you're not and then it's game over

Authenticity. Be yourself – although, obviously, the best version of you!

Integrity. Think of the people you most admire on the planet. Goodness and credibility are great cornerstones for your future.

Love. OK, I feel like I'm losing some of you now. This doesn't mean grab your interviewer with a huge embrace. I suggest you think of what makes you feel happiest, most confident, most creative – the LOVES in your life – whether that's people, pastimes, places. These are the things which make you most comfortable but also most interesting and that will ensure the image you portray to interviewers is the most (in)credible, authentic and compelling as it can be.

Treasure goes on to talk about your "vocal toolbox" and his points are difficult to quibble with. Unless you're a musician or a thespian, you've probably never thought about your voice as a toolbox. It's just your voice, right? WRONG - it's so much more than that. It's a simple fact it's not just what you say, *it's the way that you say it*. Try it out in the comfort of your bedroom. Think about the following "tools" of your voice and think about the orators you most admire and how they use their own tools.

REGISTER	Some people speak from nose or throat but experiment with speaking with more depth, from your chest. Research suggests we vote for politicians with lower voices. It might be one of the reasons why so few women have held the highest political positions…! Don't feel the need to fundamentally change your register but experiment with it. What gives you the most depth and control?
TIMBRE	The way your voice feels. Research suggests we prefer warm and smooth voices. Again, not everyone is Barry White and the colour in your voice is an important part of your personality. You may speak differently depending

	on who you're talking to – try it out
PROSODY	This one is arguably the most important for interviews. This is the rhythm, emphasis and intonation in our voices. The most engaging speakers have a colour and flavour to the way they speak but keep it simple when the situation requires it. The least effective are either monotones (i.e. speaking at one frequency no matter what you're saying) - if you do this, think about how to change it up – or those with repetitive prosody (i.e. there is intonation at the end of every sentence so every statement sounds like a question). Strip it back and think before you speak.
PACE	This is the one which most people stumble over – me included. People from certain regions in the UK with particular accents (including the Welsh accent) tend to speak pretty quickly. SLOW DOWN. And please oh please don't fear silence. Sometimes pauses in our speech are as powerful as the speech itself.

	This is the part of our speech which is the easiest to get wrong but the easiest to correct too. Practice makes perfect. Record yourself, watch it back, and see if/ how you get this right
VOLUME	This is another easy win if you work at it and, as with so many techniques you'll find in this book as with many other professional development and aspirational books – moderation and variety are the best guides. Nobody wants to be shouted at but, equally, you won't get far in this business by not being heard. Your interviewers will be experienced lawyers and/or HR professionals. They will generally be good guides to bounce off

The other big one for me is ACCENTS. I spent years at a top 6 University thinking mine wasn't the right fit for the business world. I worked hard to kick it into touch and I don't know why. When I arrived at Baker McKenzie in 2006 the firm was full of great characters from across the country – indeed – across the world with a beautiful variety of accents and glorious individual intonations in their voices. It's one of the wonderful things which make that firm so great. At Capital we're very proud to be Welsh and have a number of Welsh speakers and they sit next to people who speak Italian, German, and French, to name a few. As an interviewer I love to hear about people's journey through their lives – where they've come from and how they've arrived at their current destination. Your accent is a part of that and, I say 'embrace it'. It's also authentic and honest.

The only word of warning I would have from the millennials most likely to be reading this book (and when I say this I do so confidentiality as one of "your people" – accordingly to Wikipedia – JUST!) but please avoid slang, social media language and articulate what you want to say clearly and with confidence.

PREPARATION, PREPARATION, PREPARATION…

FAIL TO PREPARE AND PREPARE TO FAIL

It's so simple but so true. The first part of preparation is that set out above. Getting into the zone and preparing your body, your mind and your voice.

The second is your journey to the interview. I mean this literally. If you can, do a 'recce' of your interview location. Work out how you will get there, think about contingencies if certain transport fails (London-based interviews in particular – mastering the Tube is an art it took me more than a decade just to be "competent" in let alone master), and find a coffee shop (not a greasy spoon – you don't want to turn up smelling like vegetable oil) so you can hide from the elements if necessary and be ready to coolly and calmly arrive at your destination at an appropriate time – with dry and warm hands!

An appropriate time in my book is 10 minutes before you've been told to get there. The receptionist will likely show you to a waiting room. If you're planning on doing the POWER POSE ask to be shown to the bathroom and then sit down with a strong but relaxed posture for your interviewer or the receptionist to take you to the interview room. If you're looking for something to occupy your mind, pick up a legal journal or firm literature if it's available in the waiting room. Avoid newspapers as they may leave print on your hands. Try to avoid rummaging through your bag to have a last minute read through of your notes. It doesn't give off an air of preparedness or confidence for that matter.

Finally, "the Look": I'm not a fan of this topic for a number of reasons. Personally, I'm not the best person to give fashion advice. My style is fairly relaxed. I'd like to say quirky but it's probably Coco Flannel than Coco Chanel. If I know very little about women's fashion what I know about men's fashion can probably be written on a match stick. My opinion – if you want it – is that it's best to keep it simple. Clean, smart, pressed clothes. Avoid heavy aftershave, perfume or make up. I think a bit of colour is warming but I wouldn't overdo it. The same applies to jewellery for me. I often pair a simple dress with a statement necklace as I think (as we've established I'm no Gok Wan) it shows character but is smart, comfortable and, frankly, uncontroversial. You want to be remembered for the right reasons.

IT TAKES TWO (OR THREE, OR FOUR...) TO TANGO

So, to the big event...

Your application/ CV has already got you this far and so it has to be a fundamental part of your preparation for the interview. Know it like the back of your hand and explore it. You might even get a friend to ask you questions about it. Remember: it is the only thing the interviewer is going on before you turn up. If they're an effective interviewer they will have prepared questions off the back of it.

You travelled around South-East Asia in your Gap Year – where did you go? What was your favourite part and why?

You currently work in a shoe shop to help fund your studies – how do you find that? What has it taught you?

Your favourite topic at University is X – why is that? Why does it interest you? What is your least favourite topic?

How do you explain the grade you got in [INSERT] topic?

Prepare your answers to these questions and know them well. I generally use tables to record this info as it I find it an easier way to aid my short-term memory. For example:

Question	Answer	Possible connection back to firm/ job
South East Asia	I went to Thailand, Vietnam and Cambodia. It's difficult to choose but I'd say my favourite area was Angkor Wat. Watching the sun rise there was absolutely amazing.	International work – what have the interviewers done?
Shoe shop	It's a challenge working on topic of my studies but it's important to me because it gives me financial independence and it's another form of learning – working with and for people. It takes you out of the 'bubble'	Develops crucial attributes for a trainee solicitor – initiative, team-working, confidence. I hope it's another factor which will prepare me for this step…

	that University can be sometimes	

The shaded column above is the bit which I find a lot of interviewees lack. If you can do it, it makes the interviewers' jobs a lot easier because the conversation will be engaging and interesting and will move naturally from topic to topic. Think about some of the most interesting people you've ever had a conversation with or the most thought-provoking interviews you've seen on television.

Engaging interviewees don't just answer the question they're given as if it's a pop quiz. They use it to take the listener (whether that's the interviewer or an audience) on a journey. A lot of celebrities probably do it because it makes the experience more enjoyable for them. These people get asked the same questions over and over again and so who can blame them for shaking up their answers and involving the interviewers in their story? If you can do this, you'll be well placed to nail the interview because the same applies to the interviewers. They'll be asking the same sorts of questions to numerous interviewees. Firms want candidates who can give a 'global' answer to their questions. By 'global' I mean not simply someone who responds to a question as though they're taking a language test, i.e. *"What do you like about..."* with *"I like [this]...about [this]..."* but rather *"That's an interesting one. Well I really like [this] because [insert]. Don't you think...?"*

Next, the four key pillars to this sort of interview preparation:

KNOW THE FIRM

KNOW THE INTERVIEWER(S)

KNOW THE INDUSTRY

KNOW YOURSELF

I'm going to take each of these in turn but it's important to point out at such a juncture that these are not mutually exclusive. This is where having a 'global' answer is important. What do I mean by 'global'? Well, it's essentially two things: (1) applying mirror theory to your answers and (2) rounding off your answers to drive the conversation. Think of the questions that the interviewers pose as being the outline drawing – you provide the colour and you should make it as vibrant and engaging as you can – you won't be the first or last interviewee.

KNOW THE FIRM

Every firm you apply to – however big - will have a website these days. Each will likely have a "news" section which is a wealth of information. Explore it. Find the stories which most interest you and note them in your mindmap. WHY you find them interesting…?

Click on the "NEWS" tab of google to find out stories which might not have made it onto their webpage. You might get hits on BAILII (for non-lawyers – a case/ legal resource database in the UK) which tell you about recent cases the firm you're applying to have acted on (which may not be named on its site because of client confidentiality).

Or, if you want to really impress, find out the names of their published clients – you'll generally find nuggets on their websites/ individual CVs and/or legal directories like Chambers & Partners or Legal500 and then find out interesting news about that client (ideally a legal matter relating to them) and try to weave that into your answers or questions for your interviewers. Taking an example from the time of writing:

> If you're a Sports/ Formula 1 fan, a quick check of Herbert Smith's Legal500 write up in 2016/17 shows that it advised Bernie Ecclestone in his successful defence of a $145m claim brought by a German media

company. This gives rise to all sorts of questions: where you involved in the Bernie Ecclestone dispute? [If the answer is: yes..] What was he like? Fascinating man…interesting stories about him in media [there is usually an interesting story about him/ Formula 1 in the media…] etc etc

And don't forget the recurring theme in this book. The answer to most questions you are asked at interview should have a **mirror** effect: why this firm? [the answer should include why you're right for the firm…] Why you? [the answer should include why the firm…] and so on. In short, you need to get under the skin of the firm and be able to articulate why you and it/ the people are the right fit.

KNOW THE INTERVIEWER(S)

This is not rocket science and (to use a phrase I have probably over-used in this book) not knowing your interviewers is criminal. Everyone has CVs online these days (most are on LinkedIn): they give you nuggets to explore with your interviewers to make the interview as natural and conversational as possible. They'll tell you about clients they've worked with (cue the above interest in what it is like working with them/ how they operate etc), what sorts of matters they've worked on (cue google searches so you can hold a sensible conversation about what that sort of work entails), and maybe even what their interests outside of work are (maybe you have hobbies in common, for example).

The other point about CVs is that they give you the opportunity to flatter your interviewers – but don't overdo it. We all want eager candidates who are intelligent, articulate and enthusiastic. A little bit of flattery is nice: when it's clear an interviewee has done their homework on you I defy anyone not to feel a gooey sense of satisfaction inside – but don't gush too much – the interview is all about you after all.

KNOW THE INDUSTRY

The starting point for understanding the "industry" of law is, in my mind (bearing in mind, I am a public law lawyer by trade and so may be a little bit biased), understanding how we're regulated and how we're going to be regulated in the future. In fact, I'm doubly biased because one of my key clients is our regulator: the Solicitors Regulation Authority (or SRA, for short).

The SRA's website is a wealth of information about the profession, its direction of travel and plans for the future. One of the key messages (certainly at the time of writing and one I expect will continue) is innovating in the profession. This is no mean feat. We, as solicitors [warning: my view only], can be pretty old school

Knowing the industry also means knowing the business/ sectors which the firm you're applying to operates in:

- If its main bag is insurance, what is going on the insurance market? This is a really good example because technological advances (think Artificial Intelligence, automated vehicles and so on and so forth) mean that an industry with a rich history (I recently saw a video about Lloyds of London which taught me quite a lot about it) is having to think fast to not be left behind...

- If it's public sector/ health care, what is the relevant Secretary of State (or, indeed, the opposition cabinet member) saying about the future? Avoid being overtly political (you can't know the political affiliations of your interviewers), but think about potential discussion points.

- What about new legislation which has either recently been passed or what is currently going through the Houses of Parliament? I was doing my LPC when the Companies Act 2006 was coming into being and the development of this from its predecessor was a hot topic. At the time of writing, there's a lot of intrigue around the post-Brexit Repeal

Bill and how our law is going to be shaped by our exit from the EU/ how we'll deal with European developments such as the General Data Protection Regulation. Checking the progress of Bills through Parliament is super easy – just check out the Legislation Tracker @ http://www.legislation.gov.uk/new

Have a few of these in your arsenal and you're sure to impress…

KNOW YOURSELF

Put simply: know your CV/ application like the back of your hand. If you can, extend your mindmap to show connectors between your experience, achievements or interests against those of the firm you're applying to.

I said in Chapter 2 to get to know your inner narcissist and then to tame it. No one else is going to shout about how great you are. You need to master explaining to others why you're a "must employ" candidate. Finding the balance between confidence and arrogance is a life-long objective for many. Practice: ask your friends and classmates what they think. Your tutors will often be happy to help. They'll have been through this before and should be willing and able to give you constructive feedback on your approach. As awkward as it sounds, try it out in front of your mirror. Practice makes perfect.

One of the tricks to avoid the awkwardness of over-selling yourself is remembering the "mirror theory" throughout. It's much easier to explain why you're a great fit for a firm than it is simply saying that you're great!

PRESENTATIONS AND CASE STUDIES

Training contracts are super competitive. I probably don't need to tell you that: you no doubt bought this book in order to try to gain a competitive margin – however small it might be. Firms are having to get creative to find the best candidates.

I came across many a "case study" in my training contract interviews. I'll be honest with you: they're not pretty. They're often long and essay-like with some tricky questions. The good news is that, in my personal experience and from my discussions with colleagues and friends who have been through similar processes, the people interviewing you (more often than not) will want you to succeed and be there to help you.

It's impossible to set out a "once size fits all" approach for these sorts of things because every case study is different and should, in theory, be based on the sort of work you will come across if you secure a training contract with your chosen firm. But, one theme is generally consistent across all and that is: buzz words. Go through the case study and highlight key themes and words. Look for patterns in the story and they should guide you through or give you a sensible punt at any answers.

If the story you're going is going one way and then it takes a turn, think about why. It might be a red herring or might be the reason the case study was teed up on the first place. If you're like me and diagrams help you make sense of a problem, sketch out a mindmap to use during the interview with the buzz words and themes a critical part. You'll be expected to engage during the interview, not ruffle through notes, but if you can store the key points on one page, you can have that in front of you during the interview to guide you through the answers.

Non-lawyers in particular I find scorn at the prospect of being given a legal case study. I don't blame you but, don't worry, the interviewers will know that you aren't a law student and aren't expecting miracles. They're expecting some thought, analysis; reasons for your answers even if the answers aren't 'right' (sometimes there is no one 'right' answer).

The approach to answering case study questions and, indeed, putting together presentations (whether in advance of the interview or during the interview process), will generally mirror the key points for the interview itself referred to above. Think about posture, enunciation, pace… use straightforward language. There is little more off-putting than a candidate who has swallowed a thesaurus for the purposes of the interview. Keep eye contact, engage, involve, ask questions and - SMILE!

Psychometric tests are also becoming more popular. There are no cheats or tricks, but there are plenty of tools for practising this, e.g.: http://www.psychometricinstitute.com.au/Free-Aptitude-Tests.asp If you're at University, ask your tutors if your Business School (if there is one – or your Law Society or even Psychology or Social Sciences departments) if they have their own facilities.

INTERVIEWS BY SKYPE

More in vogue than ever, the application of technology does not really change the rules of the game save for two things:

1. Test the technology: try it out with family/ friends to make sure your computer, tablet, phone or whatever wonder machine you're using has the right tools to make you well understood during the interview. Make sure you have the right environment both in terms of technology and look. Generally, I would go with a plain white wall background with as much natural sunlight as you can get. You want the focus to be on you.

2. Think about whether you can/ should use the wide remit of some of these technologies during the interview. Speaking to what will predominantly be the Net Generation, this will not be lost on you but, if you want to weave in other platforms with Skype/ Facetime etc (for example, showing your Prezie or ppt in real time), check that the interviewers can receive the same platform. There's nothing like getting all the right things in place only to find technology fails you at the last moment.

AND FINALLY, HERE'S TO YOUR FUTURE!

That's it. Hopefully you found the little pearls of wisdom in this book helpful. With any luck it will have helped you make up your mind as to whether the law is right for you, what type of firm/ area of law you're most interested in, and it's given you some top tips for getting that job.

If I can leave you with one final thought, it would be this:

> *"Focus on the solution, not the problem"*
> Walter Anderson

The junior lawyers that have worked with me know this is my go-to saying. When faced with any challenge at work, I always try to do this. It's easy to be obsessed with the issue or challenge at hand, but I feel most effective when I get my energy behind finding the solution. For me, the best junior lawyers I have worked with get this pretty quickly and don't approach me with "this happened…" or "what can we do about this?" They say: "I'm planning on doing this to address that…does that work for you?"

In my mind, you should adopt the same attitude to getting your dream job. Visualise what it looks like and what it takes to get there, write it all down, illustrate it if you want – and then add the meat to these bones BEFORE you put together your application. Don't start writing until you've done this exercise. It will make your writing more structured and, more importantly, truer to you.

On that note, I have compiled my own final **MindMap (#4 in the Appendix)** for my training contract application (albeit done in hindsight now but it's a true reflection of the way I felt at the time).

Thank you and good luck!

Post script

Some top tips from those in the know…

Preparing a training contract application is like writing a story – a story about you. It needs a beginning, a middle and an end, and it all needs to hang together and make sense. Having read your application, a firm should have a strong impression of who you are – your character, desires and what makes you tick.

Alys Carlton (Partner, Capital Law; formerly a lawyer and HR professional at Allen & Overy)

When I interview candidates for a training contract I am mainly looking for the candidate to demonstrate a genuine interest in a career in the law combined with enthusiasm and a clear understanding of why he or she thinks the firm would be a good place to work.

Tom Cassels (Partner, Linklaters)

If I had to pick one alone, it would be to know the Firm you are interviewing with – do your homework, read their website, follower their social media feeds, know what distinguishes them from other firms of the same ilk, and know why you want to work for. Any sense that someone has sent a load of applications to all City firms hoping one will say yes is a massive turn off for us

Joanna Ludlam (Partner, Baker McKenzie)

Test other careers too and really work out what is is about the law that appeals. When I was interviewing applicants the people who really stood out were the ones who had done work outside law (or as different types of lawyers) and could say why they thought working in a law firm was better for them. An added benefit is that – while training contracts and legal careers are great options, they are hard work and can be all-consuming at times – when you are doing ANOTHER late night, you may be able to rest a little easier that you've made good choices!

Richard Davies (Associate Director, EMEA Litigation & Investigations at Gilead Sciences)

Get some corporate/ professional work experience, and whilst you're there, be nice, smile and show enthusiasm to everyone you meet, because you never know where your next opportunity will come from, and people are definitely more likely to recommend someone who is smiley and enthusiastic

Sarah Court-Brown (Solicitor, DAC Beachcroft)

Get to know the firm in any way possible (open days, vac schemes, events hosted by the firm at universities) because: 1. It makes the 'why our firm' question a lot easier to talk about on applications and in interview and 2. (and perhaps more importantly) YOU get to scope out the firm and get a sense of the people and culture which is important in thinking about whether the firm is a good fit for you too! It's impossible to get that from just their website

Jessica Lee (Associate, Brown Rudnick)

ABOUT THE AUTHOR

Nicola Mead-Batten is a senior lawyer at award-winning commercial law firm Capital Law based in Cardiff, South Wales. Having spent the formative years of her career at Baker McKenzie in London, Nicola has undertaken a number of secondments during her career including the Melbourne (Australia) office of Baker McKenzie, Accenture, the Professional Standards Authority for Health and Social Care, and the Merchant Navy Officers Pension Fund. She specialises in commercial litigation and public/ administrative law.

Outside of work, Nicola enjoys spending time with her young family, running and writing – this book being the first venture into publishing.

Your feedback on this book would be greatly appreciated. Please email trainingcontractbook@mail.com You can also use this address to ask the Author any questions you have about the book or the process of applying for a training contract. Nicola will do her best to get back to you but a full-time career and two children do keep her busy and so please be patient in terms of any response!

THE ULTIMATE GUIDE TO PURSUING A CAREER IN LAW AND ARMING YOURSELF WITH THE RIGHT TOOLS TO STAND OUT FROM THE CROWN IN TRAINING CONTRACT APPLICATIONS

- Starting your story
- Is the law right for you?
- The right firm
- The application
- The interview
- Here's to your future…

THE AUTHOR/ HER CREDS:

"A fantastic lawyer, former colleague and friend – Nicola, in her attitude and approach, is a great example for young lawyers (and aspiring ones) to follow" Tom Cassels, Partner, Linklaters

"This book contains all you need to know about getting a training contract– Nicola has written a deeply insightful and honest guide, sharing her experience and sharp perceptions of the challenges of embarking on a career as a solicitor". Joanna Ludlam, Partner, Baker McKenzie

"Truly remarkable and successful private practice lawyers not only possess a broad range of skills (of which knowing the law is just one), but also revel in *the opportunity to demonstrate and develop these. Nicola is one of this rare breed."* Alys Carlton, Partner, Capital Law

"When we worked together, I was constantly amazed by Nicola's focus and her ability to plan her career. I couldn't think of anyone better to give advice on how to navigate the early stages of a career as a solicitor" Richard Davies, Associate Director (senior in-house lawyer), Gilead Sciences

"Nicola was one of the nicest and most inspiring supervisors I worked for as a trainee. She is a brilliant lawyer, a lovely person and a great role model for those coming into the profession..." Sarah Court-Brown, Solicitor, DAC Beachcroft

"without Nicola's support, advice and mentoring in the first seat of my training contract, I wouldn't be the lawyer I am today. She helped me to shape my career and push it in the direction I wanted it to go" Jessica Lee, Associate, Brown Rudnick

01.

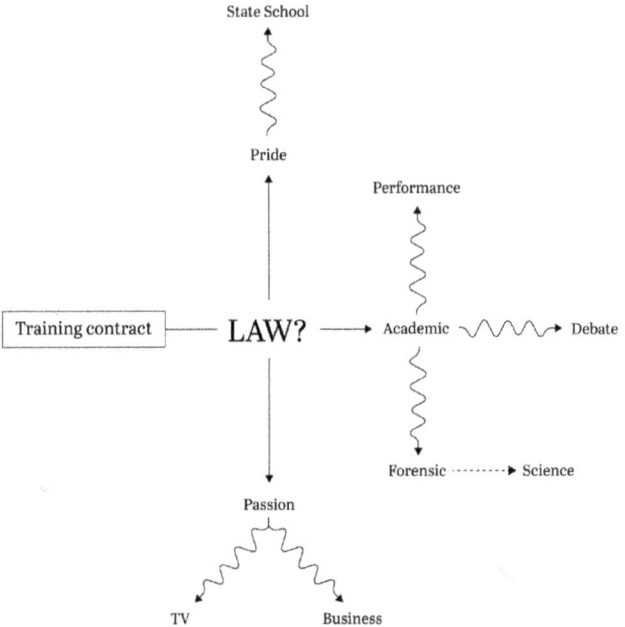

Training Contract/ Solicitor | 109

o2a.

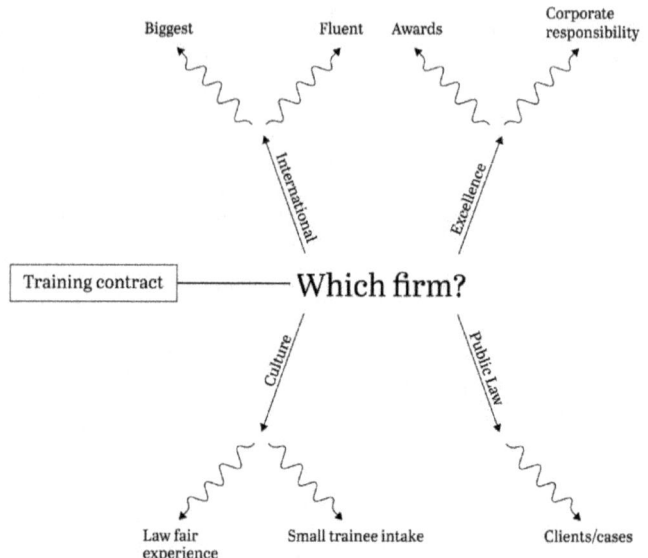

o2b.

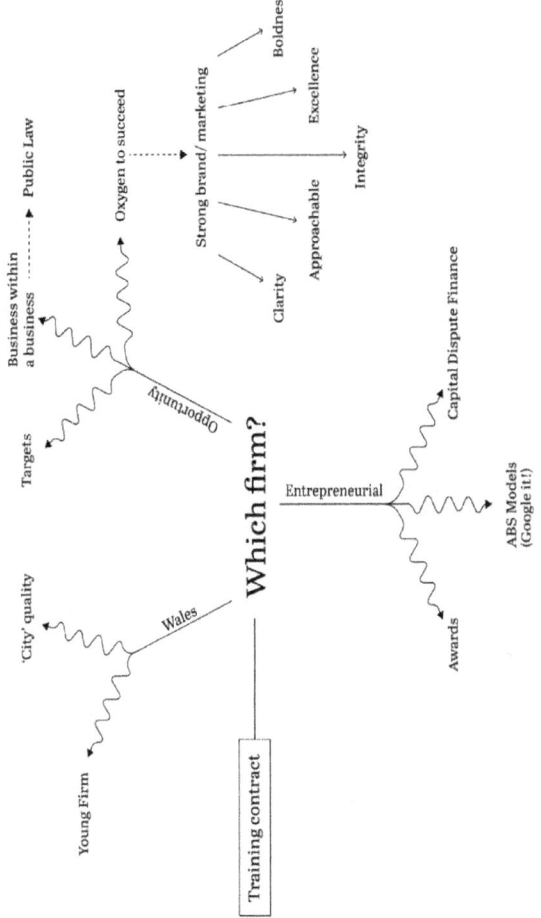

03.

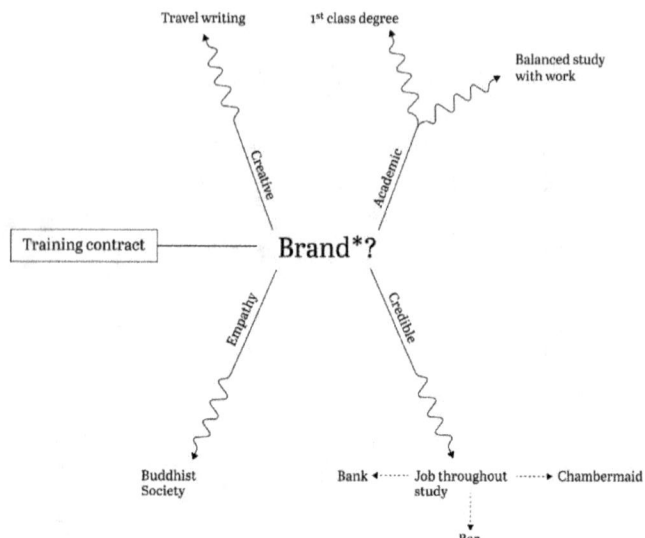

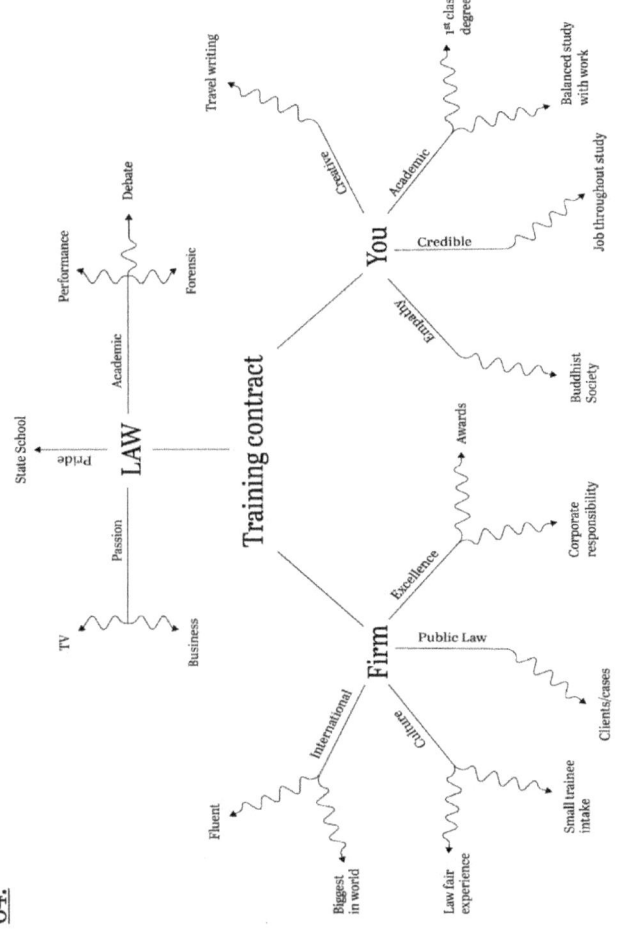

Training Contract/ Solicitor | 113

www.ingramcontent.com/pod-product-compliance
Lightning Source LLC
Chambersburg PA
CBHW050110230526
45470CB00004B/1759